Dedicated to: My Beloved Children:

Acknowledgement to: Catrina Brown for her contributions, words of loving wisdom and for being the best daughter any mother could have! This poem written for you, from your loving mother Madame "B".

SPARKLE CHILD

Whistles, bells, and sand full of pails, packed inside your little wagon;
Gentle breezes chill your delicate skin, as time goes by and you race against the wind, sparkle child.

Laughter abounds as we play outdoors, without a care in this world, hey, would anyone like to eat some chocolate smores.

Maple syrup, plums, and strawberries on top, turn the music up, its time to dance, shake, and pop, that cat there sure can groove, go! Honey, wild.

Let us see what you can do! Sparkle Child! Sing merry as you row that boat on a cloud, laughing, laughing, all the way, beautiful gemstones with brilliant hues, there is no way, that we could have the blues.

Whistles, bells, and sand full of pails, packed inside your little wagon, gentle breezes chill your delicate skin, as time goes by and you race against the wind, sparkle child!

Acknowledgement to: Brandon Brown for his contributions, comforting words, and for being the best son any mother could have! This poem written for you, from your loving mother Madame "<u>B</u>".

BEAUTIFUL RED ROSE

The red rose that never fades. Beautiful red rose, so colorful and bright, blowing in the wind all alone at night. Listening, caring for others, beautiful red rose filled with fire and might. No one who dares to look upon your beauty can help but to love you the red rose that never fades.

Beautiful red rose, so colorful and bright, blowing in the wind all alone at night. Living long, loving strong, beautiful red rose, so colorful and bright, blossomed from mother Earth to reveal the light.

Dedicated to all dear readers all over this Earth, does not matter what hue, black, white, red, yellow, or brown; that truly demonstrates how to love others.

LOVE CHOSE ME

The beauty of love surrounds the heart like the musical strings, played by a harp.

The insatiable thirst for love to feel something, anything, not to be numb with pain.

Power and might embrace our spirits like the south winds, making us worthy, telling us were to begin.

Suddenly the blue sky begins to rain, with a chill from the air; our eyes begin to open, to see the fresh morning dew.

The beauty of love surrounds the heart like the musical strings played by a harp, this kind of feeling so new, felt and chosen by a select few.

LOVE AND EMBRACE YOUR GAY CHILD

IF CHURCH OR BELIEFS SPEAK AGAINST SAME SEX

UNITY

No one ever talks about the fact, that there are millions of people in America, that do not know how to handle these types of situations when a family for years have sat in a church somewhere and when the news hit the ear waves of that congregation, that announces one of them, happens to be gay often times that person is shunned or just treated cold as ice. For example when evangelist Carlton Pearson started preaching about including everyone into the fold he was kicked out of that ministry. He had built up this place for many years. That was a big shock to so many people. I am writing these words out of love not hatred for any group I want to make that precisely clear. My intentions are to empower and to heal with words.
Loving someone that is gay cannot be wrong! Some attend church for the wrong

reasons. Many African Americans believe in their hearts that Jesus was a black man. The same very many Caucasian Americans believe that Jesus was a white man.
Some church members eat bacon each day, eating pork is an abomination in the
Bible, is it not? Thousands sing and praise then look down their nose at others.
Bayard Rustin organized the March on Washington! He did the right thing but some felt that he should have been kicked to the curb, because he was openly gay.
 I believe he should get the respect and credit for doing such a wonderful thing. The
March on Washington was his baby.

I believe that there is nothing wrong about going to church to praise the Creator of the Universe. I think that people should gently and lovingly welcome all to the fold of any congregation. Inviting each human being to come as they are.

Have you ever watched a little baby? A newborn, Just lying in their crib
crying for help for someone mother or father to come in and help them,
because they need something, even if its just to be held close for a while and
how quiet they get when you rub their little cheeks in other words, in those
moments and memories, we don't know if that little one is gay or straight
but we give our babies unconditional love. Why should we as human beings
be so cold? In addition, change that love to hatred when the child is all
grown up? I beseech you dear ones to listen to me, I am not preaching to you
I am offering a different spin on this subject. Think about someone you
know right at this moment this person may have been kicked out by parents,
sent packing by so-called friends, laughed at and joked on, dogged out, just
treated like scum of the earth! Now I understand what so many have gone
thru witnessing people say cruel things over hearing horrible words true
story I was at work in Richmond Virginia on this occasion this Caucasian
guy told a new co-worker that he was gay. At lunchtime, that same co-
worker had an audience of co-workers laughing almost as if they were in a
smoke filled room at some strange comedy nightclub. I was the only one
that did not think the jokes were funny. I'm sure people out there in the
world probably have seen it all and will not be shocked by this but you had
to be there to see the look on that guy's face he was so embarrassed, and
anybody with a heart could see how hurt he was. At that time I didn't know
anyone or that guy but I tried to help him I tried to make that other guy back
off. I understand that some people in this world will always believe that its
right to hurt instead of healing one another because we all have some type of
scar on us somewhere. I believe in loving people, all people that show me
any form of kindness, I tell people I can see thru them, what I really mean is
that I can sense what kind of heart that they have, because after you have
experienced pain yourself, you know what it feels and looks like, on a face
when a spirit has been broken inside of any person, gay or straight. My
heart says yes! Yes! Help that hurting individual feel better if you can I feel
it is my duty to try to help them. Loving someone that is gay or someone
that is different is not a sin it's your duty to love that person take them under
your wing try to protect them from harm. In addition, to all the self-
righteous hypocrites out there, I can hear your judgment in your statements;
most of them are not righteous. Because a righteous person has the
intelligence to know not to dare say that, another person is going to hell.
How do I know that person is going to hell! Only the Creator of the universe
can say that! I'm the type of person that would not have the audacity to boast
about anything, because we all are imperfect beings shaped and molded into
the person our Creator wants us to become, takes an awful lot of grace and

time to get where we're going. I am just grateful that God do not give up on us. The way we give up on ourselves, forgiving us over and over again. Just sit down a moment and think about all the wrong that you have done in your lifetime, anyone should quickly be made aware that you are a walking miracle, we are blessed. Loving someone is not a sin, let me reiterate! Loving someone that is gay is not a sin. When people adopt a child and raise that child as their own. Do they say this child is not mine when that same child grows up and say mom or dad I'm gay. They have loved and nurtured this child always. Should they stop now? No wait answer this question! Should they stop loving that child? My answer is no. they should continue to love that child, think about that little boy or girl that was so sweet with obedience and mannerable to everyone that came for a visit, she playing with her friends, he being so playful. Interviews with parents that I have met, when some would tell me that their child was gay, they would burst into tears afterward, especially in the African-American community. Therefore, I would try to console them and maybe my tactics were wrong because immediately I became angry and would yell at them something like, what is wrong with you! Do you realize what you are saying? I am going to pour a bucket of cold water on you! If you do not stop talking like that! Think about all the horrible things that your child could be doing! You need to give your child your all! That is your duty as a parent or caregiver. Just give them your all because think about all the abusive language and the cruel behavior they will have to endure because unbelievably, there are some very heartless, demented, ignorant folks living in America. In addition, if you have not met any of them believe it one day you will. Your child needs love and a place to come home to where there will be peace and quiet in an loving atmosphere, when a gay person comes out they will have to hold on and go through the fire out there in this world, because there will be mean things, hurtful things said and done to them. Remaining strong will be a challenge for that persons family, or for that gay son or daughter believe it people go after them, family members also, there are many acts that are considered detestable and vexed. Some people have said that a grown man or woman raping a little boy or girl is the same as two gay people being together! When I heard this statement, I almost fell over from pure shock! I am not gay but if I was, that statement would have made me even more furious. What do raping innocent little children have to do with two gay people that genuinely love one another? We all must think about sowing good seeds and when we do right then righteousness will follow. To most of us, our children are our biggest accomplishments, our pride and joy, we hold on to those facts of our lives like money in the bank. Should we start withdrawing our love instead of giving it? On the other hand, should we save our love only for special occasion or holidays when our gay child comes to visit? I believe in love and what love brings with it, reaching out an extending your arms. Most people in return will not fight it; they will just hug you back even if you have just met them. I have hugged many people I did not know, just introduced myself and started hugging them. Moreover, believe it they enjoyed it as well. We all need love to survive in this life. We all want to feel, see it, and touch it, that is why people still like to see themselves in a photograph, because sometimes you can see and feel the love from just one picture. Loving someone that is gay is not a sin. Why do some people expect us to stop loving our child? To all those people, I say are you kidding! My child that I birthed into the world labor pains and all, the same little child that would constantly say I love you! I love you so much. How can anyone just say you are to leave my house and never come back! Well my heart cannot and will not allow me to utter those words to anyone that I love. That is why I believe that it is not a sin to love a gay person. There is not much that shocks me anymore but I have heard people say it is a sin to love someone that is gay. That is one of those demented, ignorant people that I was talking about earlier. The same one that some of you out there, will run across. When it happens, it can be someone you have known for years that you did not even know felt that way. That type will hit below the belt their main mission is to make you hurt and suffer. My response is to stand up, walk right up on them close, look them straight in the eye and defend your child, sister, brother, mother or father. I think that will put an end to some of this cruelty. There has been an uproar about our President Barack Obama being biracial, well I even heard people in restaurants talking about the white woman that gave birth to him and this was on Mother's day at that! My response is, I thank God for the white woman that gave birth to him, because otherwise we would not have our President. I do not see why people are shocked, there will always be white women that will fall in love, sleep with a black man and have his babies. The only difference is in the 21st century it's not hidden behind closed doors like it use to be and thank God for that. The same way there has always been gay people out there. They are just fed up, tired of hiding in the closet, and in my opinion, I would rather that you tell me the truth that you are gay then pretending that you are not. Now I believe gay people are more responsible and more professional. They need to continue to be who they are! Do not pretend or be on the down low, which is not cool! I watched a movie once the man in the movie had been married for 20 years and had grown children, when his secret came out his family was devastated. They worked it out in the ending. Let me tell you a true story I have had over 100 jobs and on this particular job, I was the new person, innocently speaking one day. I said I really like to see Ellen come out dancing the way she does on her show. This vicious person started a rumor that I was gay and afterward people started to treat me differently. I was so hurt how dare this mean heifer! Do this to me! I thought about confronting the person but why should I? People are going to believe what ever they want anyway. I just moved on, I made this point to let you all see the power of words and what those words can do to alter someone's life. Take this really famous wealthy lady that has a nontraditional relationship with her boyfriend, the way they've been together for years and years and remain together instinctively. I believe that if that love can last its only because the love there, is the purest love. The kind of love that will make two people be there and do what it takes to make each other happy or joyous so you can live a peaceful life without all of that stress that comes along with always wondering about what people think of you, or your relationship. Gay people need to feel safe, and free to live, work and play in America without the fear of being bullied by some fanatical person, that gets their jollies from hurting people. Using God for an excuse to belittle, and humiliate another person when they are trying to live peaceful not bothering a soul, why then some people think it is o.k. but I am here to say it is not o.k. What I'm trying to say here and now is, do not wake up the sleeping lion that you really don't want to mess with, and be logical instead of judgmental. Am I going to hell because I like to dance and have two cocktails per day? My Creator knows I enjoy dancing and sipping a glass of wine on occasions. Some people or just evil and there is no color or size attached to evil-minded people. And sad to say that they are not going anywhere no time soon, this type have been here since we got smart enough to record time. Well you might be thinking about a time in your life when someone bullied you or maybe you witnessed someone else getting some type of abuse and that person was straight. Should we the people be so blind to think that in our culture its o.k. to abuse the little boy or girl that grows up to be gay and when we can see where that person heart is, just as loving and kind as can be. Should we continue to work and interact in our communities and treat them wrong? I know this statement might offend some people but I have to say it again. There is nothing wrong and it is not a sin to love someone that is gay. Americans love to divide and put labels on human beings, take a look at this experiment a group of adults are sitting in a focus group, talking smiling getting along fine until this C.E.O. comes in and tells them to identify each person that's knocks on the door entering the room. Then here comes the labels and division some said that person is African-American even if some was actually Latino or from the Middle East and other countries, some would say that man right there has to be gay look at how he's dressed wearing a pink shirt or lime green suit, but that man is straight. Also just because a woman shaves her hair to a clean cut does not mean that she is gay. Here are just a few examples of how ridiculous some people think about this issue. We live in multi-cultural societies, How did this happen? Once I took, a book to work did not think anything of it since I love to read and write books, the book was called 'The Confessions of Nat Turner." The supervisor at that time saw the book and went ballistic and started a rumor that I was a racist and nothing could be farther from the truth! I just wanted to know what happened at Nat Turner's trial! It was just one of many books that I have read, I tell you one thing, I have never been more furious in my life! Because I believe that the only reason he did that to me is because he thought I was gay, since I was in fact the only female working with a bunch of males that had chauvinistic attitudes towards women! They seem to believe the notion that she must be, because why is she working with us, that started happening more often after I confided in one of them that was in the church every Sunday, that I had a family member that I loved dearly that was gay. So now, you begin to see clearly it's not just the individual that has to endure the foolishness at the hands of some of the simple-minded people, like I said sometimes it's the entire family. Oh yes its gotten better in the 21st century but still I am sure if I could reach out touch all the people across America, some would agree with me and had similar situations in their own lives happened to them. If I had multiple phone lines all of them would be lit up right now. For years, I have suffered in silence and I'm sure many God fearing people has also. The religious aspect of being gay in America is still a touchy subject because to some it on the same page as death .Many families will not discuss this subject the same way some will not talk about death. This is one example of statements I made while working in St. Louis, Missouri. "I am not trying to be a man!" I am working trying to put food on my table! And pay my bills. Now most African-Americans are loving kind hearted people that will embrace and welcome anyone into the family unit. Race is not a issue when it comes down to the judgment factor. Many people that believe in God very strongly simply will not change their view on the same sex issue. Many believe that if they give in on this issue then their whole world around them will come crashing down. When the smoke clears, people from that same faith or congregation will confront them one by one and crush them to dust, with Bible verses. Most often taken out of context, to use against a set of individuals, which has not harmed them in anyway. Let me tell you a thing

or two about church folk. I have over 40 years experience in dealing with
the kind of church folk that pretend to be hallow driven. Which is to say
doing everything under the sun that is considered wrong then every time the
church door opens, they flock to them in droves? This is the real truth once,
I was trying to be on time for the Easter Sunday service, when the usher
escorted me over to this particular pew the lady that was seated, shouted to
both of us with a combative look, and demeanor "you better not bring
anyone else over here!' The usher was just as shocked as I was. I had not
attended this church before and had not been to church in a long while.
Since she was a big spender in that church, she was trying to tell all the
ushers what to do. Since I was not a member just visiting, I never went back.
I want people out there to really get what I am saying. When I left the house
that Sunday morning I thought, I looked decent but I believe when she
eyeballed me, she looked at my dress and she really looked at me from head
to toe. I believed   I was dressed nice, but no I couldn't afford designer
Labels and shoes at that time, But I do pay good money for clothes and I
also sew my very own designs, Many women have paid me to tailor make
my 18th century inspired designs. Right then and there I realized that there
was nothing godly about her nasty behavior. Actually I was a little sadden
by her attitude towards me and I'm only speaking about the kind of church
folk that will make another person shed tears. Once I tried to join the choir at
this church here in Montgomery ,Alabama and this member a male said to
the rest of them he wanted my spot because some of them really seem to
enjoy my audition so I did not join after he made such a fuss. I told him he
could have it! Granted there are some great hard working, kind, loving
church folk with their heart fixed for God, out there in this world, in our land
called America that we love so dear. Make no mistake about that ,those are
the ones that you can see clearly in the most unlikely places some are the
down trodden, that may not have much, but are thankful for what they have,
the ones that smile anyway, when things are going wrong, most of them
have beautiful smiles. They do not walk around the church, in front of
everyone looking like they have been sucking on a lemon, since God knows
when! I am not shame of who sit beside me in any church in America or
where ever I am! How dare we complain about that in the churches! Another
time over the years since I have lived in different states and traveled all
across America for real this is the God honest truth. Once I took myself and
my children to this church that was all one race of people in Springfield,
Missouri and the minister came and found me and I quote "Are you all lost?"
I said no this church was closest to my home so I just decided to come and
check it out. He made it very clear to me that we were not welcomed there,

another traumatizing moment in my life but I told him that I would not be back but we will stay to hear his sermon, really I forgot what he preached about, or I blocked it out! I thought we all were welcomed to any church in this world. I guess I was wrong! So when people ask me why you don't attend church every Sunday I tell them I attend church the same way I settle my taxes at the end of the year, I make a big deal of making sure I go to church to give thanks to God. I, do not pick a certain date I just go between December and February, after that, I turn around and wait to the next year. Many people have told me that I am wrong for that, but so far, I have not had any problems. Because I believe the Creator of the universe looks at what is inside your heart. Out of the abundance of the heart the mouth speaks. There is no rule that says I must be there every time the church door opens. I think people use church for therapy or something else but for me by grace I give and write these words, always each day giving thanks in prayer to the creator of the universe for everything even when trouble and storms come and believe me I have had many. When you move up in the ranks and truly become a prayer warrior, you will see that the Creator of the universe will move mountains for you. Many say that evolution is the way to go. I believe in creation because being an artist and loving arts and crafts, I believe that if we just take a moment and look around everything we are wearing, sitting on, riding in, talking on and so on someone had to have the mindset and received the idea to create these things. Things that does not grow from the ground. Can I get a witness out there? Do not give up on what you believe. We all make a wrong turn sometimes. My children and I know what it feels like to beseech the creator for help because it does not matter how much money, fame or degrees you have, something will happen to you unexpectedly that will make you pray and fall down on your knees make you do it, breathed the life back into you, when you feel like there is no hope. I do not believe in being a hypocrite because I want to be pleasing in the sight of my Creator so that I will welcome in the spirit of the goodness of God, to accompany me everywhere I go. Does that mean I can be perfect? No, why should someone telling them that their perfect accept such a bold compliment, a woman told me that once when I was in my twenties she was much older than me and she had me trying on her old outfits that she had fond memories of . She had a nice house in Rochelle, New Jersey and she said she paid a lot for those clothes. I went ahead and played along until she told me that I looked perfect, then she said I was perfect! An elder man that entered the room that was a boarder, she asked him the perfect question. So I had to stop her because she kept on saying it, I am not perfect I said very gently. She replied Oh you are! Then my voice got a little bass in it, I said I believe it is a sin for anyone to say that they are perfect when the scriptures clearly tell us that we all are born imperfect and that was the end of that! I was living in New Jersey at that time on for real she would try to drill that into my head. Nevertheless, I could not let her. Now back to the issue at hand being gay in America has been a bumpy road for some people if you are gay, your family accepts you with open arms that is just fantastic, and more love towards you. Since I have had the patience to endure the heartaches and pain from listening to a gay family member. I just want people to know that there is someone that you can go to and confide in if you are one of the ones that has been rejected by relatives or whoever they may be out there, that is giving you grief. I am saying that you can be yourself around me as long as there is love and respect for one another. Let me testify this day please hear every word I say on the subject that has caused so much pain and grief for millions of people not knowing who to trust or confide in, keeping secrets that will not do none of us any good just be yourself! Do not pretend because sometimes you bring anguish on your life and stress by pretending, this scenario is a fact it truly happened. Some people cruelty is breathtaking and I am very grateful I am not cruel to anyone gay or straight. I like to have manners it makes life a little easier for example back in the 80's when HIV first appeared on the scene many clients of mine would come into my place of business saying how afraid they were of it and how gay people should be ashamed of themselves. This particular morning I turned the open sign around 8:59 am right after I ate my breakfast then suddenly the door open and there stood a man, I had never met before he sat down after a very loud good morning! When I looked in his eyes I could sense something was terribly wrong, I gently asked him, may I help you? Is there anything wrong? The floodgates opened wide he could hardly contain himself, he started to weep bitterly. This man was an African-American male that appeared to be in his forties and I was a business owner in my twenties at that time, not knowing what to do I said to myself Lord tell me what to do! I stared at him in amazement his cries melded with the jazz on the radio, still I could not block out the sound of his agony so I turned the sign around again to say closed and locked the door. My heart aching from the vision of this good-looking grown man weeping uncontrollably. I just held him and let him get it all it out of his system. While I whispered it's going to be alright, it will get better. Afterward there was a long pause of silence then he would start weeping again it was almost as time stood still, look at me holding and rocking back and forth this stranger, tears started to roll down my cheeks as, I'm thinking Oh Lord what is happening? Still frantic, I managed to walk over to the soda machine and buy drinks for the two of us, here I said drink this it will make you feel better. Would you like something to eat? No he replied softly, After he finished his soda he started to speak, first he apologized for causing such an uproar, then he told me that his roommate had put him out of the house, that they shared for over 5 years, and he didn't have any money in his savings, his voice quivering he started to sweat, he said I can't believe this has happened to me. I have no place to live, I am homeless! I have been living a lie, hiding it very well until the day before yesterday I forgot about it and left a letter from my lover on the kitchen table that revealed we were in love. He said he heard it through the grapevine to come here from another client of mine. I became so complacent I started to believe my web of lies but when my roommate confronted me with rage in his eyes, we struggled, there could have been a bloody fistfight but I got out of there he said. I probably will have to have the National Guard by my side to get my things. Right at that moment, I became very angry. No! You will not! I blurted out! I will help you, my big mouth and me. I am thinking to myself what have I done! Now I am concerned of how much this is going to cost me! At that point I didn't worry about it, I just gave him the money for a deposit and I held my breath until he told me that he had found a place but the deposit was only $300 but he would not have it until his next pay period, and also money for food to last him a couple of weeks. I could take an exhale of relief, then because I had over $500 in my purse from the day before business was good leading up to a big holiday so I did not think on it just prayed on it and gave him $500. I prayed, Lord I believe that I will make this money back so I'm going to just give it to him, I just couldn't stand to see any one homeless at Christmas time ,and these are a few of the words I told him as I handed him the money. I give you this money that I've worked hard for with love in my heart for you and the situation that you're going through you do not have to ever pay me back! His mouth flew open as he smiled brightly. Thank you! Thank you! He just kept on saying thank you! After I shampooed his hair, he kisses me on the cheek and started out the door. I said remember the money is a gift but you can come back to see me anytime and it wouldn't hurt my feeling if you would call or write me to let me know how you're getting along. He shook his head yes smiled, then said I promise I will, two weeks later I received a big bouquet of flowers from him the card read. Thank you very much from the man that cried in your arms. I still wish I had that card, and yes, I did make three times the $500 in the following two weeks I am very thankful for being able to do such a kind deed for someone that was truly suffering! You might be sitting in a church right now right next to your gay child that you love the same as the rest of your family wondering what other family members are going to think when they find out the truth. Lord give me strength I always say! We need to keep remembering that we are not doing anything wrong by loving and caring for someone that is gay. I truly love my gay kinfolks and I do not judge them. I am more interested in knowing are they doing all right, the mother in me comes out. Have you been eating? Are you having safe sex? Is it safe in the neighborhood you are living in? I do not worry about the rest all I want them to be is loved. That is my main goal I want them to feel that they are loved. A relative told me that they had a problem with the word happy, joyous is the word they really like the most. When I asked why? The reply was that "happy is a state of mind that most people never reaches." Well I try to always look on the smooth chocolate side of life because multitudes enjoy a box of exquisite chocolate the real thing! Our Creator has years of experience in judging all the creations of the earth this world as we know it. We do not have to worry about meeting some quotas "you just have to qualify" and it is very easy to qualify by measuring the love that is inside of our hearts. Showing everyone love, dignity, and respect assures that most will return the compliment. Always try to experience life pleasantly because many parishioners do not like joy or peace. Isn't hating others a sin? Do we worship for our souls? Are we trying to compete with each other over clothes and money? I do not believe that the true Messiah is pleased with that! Like most religious people and the early missionaries that were aware of the alienation and the grave enormous injustices inflicted on the indigenous people and the millions of human beings that were killed and violently uprooted and shipped to another land to be bought and sold. All the information hidden for hundreds of years from people that could not speak the language of the land to be oppressed and confused about their birthright and heritage. We need to meticulously examine the facts of history when we question numerous subjects concerning basic human rights. Count all the lives of little children that were cut short by the holocausts this blatant sin of humans against humans. The way the story goes is that there were many challengers of the church and some of the crusades in history had little to do with God or religion. The many victims of in the name of God, I will commit the horrific tragedies according to the principle of faith, shameful reoccurring that influences our life today. Monumental crimes committed and lead by people who were baptized, with the use of organized religion denied victims basic human rights.

Using religion for their very own lascivious lusts! What do raping little children, turning those children into silent traumatized accoutrements have to do with God! Check history of the entire world out, if you can bear to read the truth. I have shed many tears over this! Matter of fact I am crying right now. I cannot help it; I thank my God my Creator for blessing me with a heart that cares. The truth has been hidden for hundreds of years not until the new technology that the 21st century offers so abundantly, the truth is staring at us all eye to eye and the information is available for the whole world to see. A lot with be knocking but will not be able to get in! The Creator of the universe is not blinded by human puffery, only by grace and mercy we are alive and witnessing the future and the years to come. We cannot deny what has happened in the past but we do possess the knowledge to change this earth make it a healing place instead of a hurting ground. Acknowledging the facts in my opinion is a way to start to heal. In truth and humility with all sincerity should we embrace our

Gay populations we should not turn our noses up or point the finger of blame. Being born and raised in the south, sometimes especially at night, when the wind is blowing, gust pounding in the breezes. I lie there still in my bed to listen to the sounds coming from the wind, it almost sound like protracted crying and wails of little children. I know that some will beg to differ but when we love and become a more loving individual everything and everyone around us can feel that loving presence. Decipher and respond to this question. If you and your family visited a new church, would you feel safe in a room filled with violent predators or gay people? In addition, there is the kind of person that as soon as they get a promotion the ego becomes inflated and they start treating people like dirt and they do not have to be famous, they can make your life miserable on a job just because they have the power to do it. I think that too is a form of violence.

Being violent in America is common now days, you only have to turn on the T.V. to see that women are fighting, men are fighting, children are posting fights they have had on the internet, to show the whole world, what are we thinking? That is not cute, there is nothing nice about violence, what are we doing to our country? What are we teaching the next generation? Granted, anyone needs to defend himself or herself but sensationalism has taken it to a new level of unbelief. Two of the most important things in America should be education and healthcare. America needs to try to stay strong in the future. When there is a lot of violence and shocking behavior how can we advance as a nation when every one out there is trying to, out shock each other and the public is getting addicted to it. What can humanity do to save the future? I can sum it up in one word "change" start with the person in the mirror set the example for others. There are so many that have money but do not know what to do with it and so many students that are college material but hardly can afford to go, with education comes sanity and knowing ones history and family roots. which I believe all people in this world would benefit from knowing the truth.

When Americans realize that love is not to be taken for granted because there are so many people I've encountered in my life that have said "I grew up in a broken home where there was no love only violence." Moreover, these were church folks! I ask you where is the love for our gay brothers and sisters in the congregations across America. Then we wonder why some want to get as far away from Christianity as they can. How can anyone watch someone that is so homesick and in tears, because they have been just put out of the house with nowhere to go. This happens a lot in African-American homes because some parents are not given the tools to handle this subject well. Come on I need some worshipers that can give me an Amen, because they know it is the truth. Just because a child turns 18 that do not mean that, they're ready to face this big treacherous world all alone, a child that is so delicate and pure so innocent in their hearts needs guidance and the wisdom from elders in order to succeed. Prayer really does change things and that

child can have a productive life, give them tools along with memories that no matter what comes their way in life no one will be able to pull them apart from the compassion for others. Always remember where the Lord has brought them up from. There is a lot of anger in most families now a days all sorts of problems, the thing is, anger or hatred won't change a thing but love will. Love is the answer to a broken spirit. Embrace that love with one of yours show them some kindness even if you have to start out in small steps to build up to the point that you can remove some of the awkwardness to let that person know without a shadow of a doubt that they are indeed worthy of love. Hold that person's hand the power of touch is amazing in the seasonal storms of life. Start to nourish that relationship by giving freely like natures replenishing rain. You might be a parent that has just discovered your child is gay and right now, you might be feeling shattered and weak about the news!

That is natural especially if that child had made up stories or kept it hidden from you but believe me it is not the worst thing that could happen. You might be afraid for their safety, safety is a big concern and rightfully so then you might be thinking "what about my grandchildren" but you can heal and get through all of that the most important part of it all is not losing contact with your child because that will hurt you more in the future. Having that child in your life is very important because being gay in America is not easy. Each year we all hear stories of people that want the right to live a productive life and these headlines are hard to escape. Consider mending that broken relationship try hard with all your might so when the day comes or if conflict arise you can honestly sit back and say "I tried my best" to keep my family together. You do not have to be the one that turned your back on your gay child, come to a comfortable agreement that benefits the whole family. The Lord is everlasting and will always be there letting us know what to do next. We can handle this.

Once I heard this story as told to me by a gay young man. He said that he had met a young man that was gay he was 13 when his family found out that he was gay, during that time he didn't know what to do he was in so much turmoil inside, his father had a violent temper even though he was a deacon in the church. He said his father did not hesitate to beat him senseless, he said he cried out for help but no one else in the family came to his defense. While his father punched him like he was a grown man but he was just a child. "Daddy please don't kill me" he kept crying out but he survived when he was kicked out of the house. Twenty years went by, someone in the family did send him an invitation to his family reunion one year, now being a fully-grown man "maybe things have changed," he thought. He attended the reunion dressed in drag to get back at the family for turning their backs on him. They knew who he was sitting there beautifully dressed but not one of them came over to even say hello they avoided him like he was a being from some unknown planet. And all the hurt and pain,

From his past started to surface again until he could take it no longer and left. That had to be traumatizing, at a family reunion how ironic. However, I wish he would have had the determination to confront them and stand up and fight for his right to be there. Now if I could have had the chance to be his friend or advisor, I would have cautioned him not to attend dressed in drag. After all, they had not seen him in years and I think that he should have carefully thought that part through, because considering the facts and how they felt about same sex unity; I believe that by him dressing in drag opened up old wounds for the family as well. He sitting there dressed in drag might make some church folks think he has made his choice. "He has chose hell and not Heaven" so lets move on. Honestly, some church folks are bold enough to make a huge call about another human being soul. Considering the scripture that say that we are all predestined, shouldn't the Creator of the universe make that call about creatures of the earth? A new approach is eminent.

When we live our lives expressing love and having a giving spirit then we tend to receive a sense of purpose after all there has to be another reason that we all are here. The facts are there is a future for all of us in America and the rest of the world. Humankind has the power within to change the direction of this world, giving back to the earth, nourishing the earth and repairing the earth to as close as it can get to its original beauty and splendor. Purifying the food and the air we breathe is a great start, but there is more to be done. Having love being the center of any task is a wonderful blessing to behold.
 Celebrate the ideas of having health and well-being for our entire family by remembering that it does not matter what position or what status or image you portray it is true that from the dust, we were formed and to the dust, we shall return. Thereby living each day doing unto others with hope and sincerity is a great blessing for all humankind to strive for which in turn will make the earth smile again. With the blessing and truth from our Creator that holds the power to bring forth bread from the earth.

Always giving thanks and being thankful for the little or the lot that we have. Reminding ourselves that there is someone out there somewhere that does not even have running water or electricity. Things that we take for granted each day, the Creator is the holy being that gave man these ideas to invent these things. We cannot take credit for our inventions because our brains are the control tower of our bodies but we still need to follow directions to get to where we are going or where we want to go. Now let us talk about how some people will try to use religion to control a group of people particularly the gay communities, now let us lay it all out on the table we know that some say that they are born that way. Some say that they have changed and are willing to try not to be attracted to the same sex by prayer. Then you have people that were molested as a child so they say they were led into it and it is a learned behavior. There will always be controversy surrounding this subject and I do not think it will be settled until the Messiah comes back and settle it for the last time. Abraham a beloved of the Bible told the Pharoah, his wife was his sister because he did not want to be killed. David another beloved committed murder but he was forgiven by the Almighty the Great I Am. There are many situations that we will never be able to understand mysteries will remain in our surroundings. Speaking to our gay sisters and brothers in America whenever you do come across someone that's being abusive just walk away if you can, because I've heard stories of how this one young man beat his mother really badly because she was being abusive toward him. There is nothing in this world that my Mother or Father could say to me that would make me raise my hand to strike neither of them. Even if it is abusive words coming from the parent's just leave walk away, two wrongs do not make a right. When someone tries to push, you to that point just get out of there until you cool down. Be very careful in your speech and how you approach the parents or loved ones because it is a big deal to some. Gently tell them your news so that the family will have a chance to digest it.

Digesting the news my, my, my, that is a difficult task for many families to deal with even in the 21st century. We're living in a time where multitudes are saying that there turning over their life to the lord, living with depression, and high job losses are just a few of the challenges we face. We will deal with those issues too and this gay stigma still lingers in just about every state. We are a people of proud heritages and cultures. Life is a gift to be here to live and work and play is something to be cherished. Digesting your child's sexual orientation should be the least of our worries but it is understandable to be concerned especially since you hear and read about the horror stories about men, women, and children being murdered for being gay! That is what I am talking about! That needs to stop! In addition, Americans need insist this type of behavior be dissolved. Church folks are usually caring people so why is this matter so hard for some to stand up and tell the people yes I do have a gay child. Should I just stop loving my child for that reason? My child has a lot to offer to society and I will love my children until the day I die!

Some church folks need to get their own house in order before the self-righteous ones can do some good. Instead, I have met many people that will say bitter harmful words in the same breath that they are professing to be of God! Generations today are under so much pressure and with all the choices today, we all are overwhelmed. The images we see and what I am writing about is the pain and agony of negative dialogs. As a Mother I would much rather my child come and tell me openly that their gay than to lose my child to suicide. The doors of communication should be left open always. Reaching out to your child delivers solutions to issues that are hard for human beings to digest. Some people are so selfish and full of themselves to the point that even if a parent is desperately extending the lines of communication it should be lovingly returned. It is a two Way Street forget about mistakes of the past and most important forgive so you can live in peace. Following the true Messiah, I am a firm believer in an eye for an eye, when I told a co-worker that I slept better at night when President Obama killed Bin Laden some were outraged How can you condone murder?

My response (why should one person think that they should continue to live after killing thousands of innocent people. Caught by surprise unaware of what was about to happen to them. Whatever the person name that did that terrible act should expect to be taken out. Do I believe that if someone is sitting on a park bench they should be shot to death by some jerk driving by? No, I do not! Because that could happen to anyone, I believe that if a person, does not matter if their black, white, red, yellow, or brown, gay or straight if that person is minding their own business. Not concerned about the neighbor across the street from them, and if that same neighbor take it upon themselves to walk across the street to your house and you never have met this person, If they start an altercation at your house, well they deserve to get that ass kicked. They brought that altercation to your house therefore; I believe that they asked for it. When some people do things like that they really do not know what your situation is, you could have just been released from the hospital.

They did not know and did not care about anyone but themselves and some of them be on something. My understanding of living in peace means that we all need to do unto others treat all with dignity and respect that is what loving others is all about. If humans could learn that there would be less crime in the world. I believe in loving family and loving our country after all this land is where most of us was born and raised, where we want our children to grow and our grandchildren to grow up in this great big pot of gumbo. Melting pot of many cultures, America needs to be protected for our loved ones sake. The generations that will face many roadblocks along the way. Dear hearts we must unfold that inevitable truth. We all have a soul, "Does any man know how to separate a soul?" Profound questions will always be collected in this era. Many have become disillusioned along with sorrows. Living strong and having longevity is a choice that the human brain positively responds. There will always be fruits of the spirit that mankind cannot buy.

America has the ability to set the example for the rest of the world. Showing other countries that the citizens of America, love peace instead of war. Set the example I always say. Let all the invisible immigrants come to the table find a solution to the situations as hand. We all know every conflict can be solved if humans would just compromise willingly to find the answers. Some church folk have the praise part right along with perfect attendance. Still the heart is not right in some because love is the first commandment, the power of love can change this world into a bright future. Democracy and freedom from the heart of America being thankful for what we do have in our land, so newcomers can be deeply moved. Greed is the ingredient that has mixed the minds of multitudes. I have heard some in the pulpit say, if we could just build a bigger church we could take in more money. What do you think? Do you believe that the Creator of the universe is pleased with that statement? What does money have to do with gently welcoming a wounded soul into the congregation of the church? I thought I had seen and heard it all working on 100 jobs along with self employment business I've ran, but

That really did shock me. Out of the abundance of the heart the mouth speaks. Its getting redundant out there with phrases like "slap two people and tell them this or that" I understand the gesture but what does high fiving people or slapping as they call it has to do with bringing people together? Once I attended a church I speak the truth about it, this lady got up and sang a solo, I'm thinking how nice until she didn't sit back down she sang song after song after song until the Pastor stood up and preached about 15-20 minutes along with a few of the phrases in his sermon, took collection up then sent everyone on their way. Unbelievable being a visitor, oh I am thinking I did not come here to be amused or entertained. I came here to hear the word. Afterward the whole congregation barely spoke got in their fine cars and left. Sad to say but I did not visit there again. Later I asked around about that church, this man said, and I quote "lady you went to a dead church? You can hardly get those folks to say amen and if I were you I would go elsewhere." What do you think about that? Talk about being flabbergasted.

Churches can be legendary for being the "dead church" when you are treated as that just turn it over to the Lord. Enjoy state of the art peace honey you will live longer and your spirit will get stronger and stronger and harder to break. The old folk use to say " when you buy sense no one can take it away" in other words when you learn from experience it was you who went through that encounter and now you are strong because you were the one that felt that, saw that and heard that. It is amazing to me where I hear the split-level ridiculousness how non-resourceful. The most universal singular thing we do in this world is worship. Dearly beloved, I beseech you to remember that we are mere mortals and life is not promised to us except eternally. Sacrificing to help others should be one the main goals of the church not giving in to the pressures of this world. Worshipping apart segregated from one another. Do you think that is right? Just because a person is in the ministry to me that does not mean that person should try to consume

control another human being. Because I have met many that have tried to use me for no good in the name of the Lord. Our different views should bring us together not tear us apart. Some church folk become miserable and mean when their offspring confides in them about their sexual orientation. I believe that some has never had the opportunity to be introduced to common sense or sensitivity. We are still suffering from a shameful, painful past in our nation. We need to show that Americans can be more caring, kind and loving toward each other all the time not just when a disaster happens. When we can love and not pretend to be those just say no to everything felons sitting in a gallery full of people filled with flaws. I asked a church member to which was a co-worker at the time to name some of his faults since he was so great at telling others and me what ours were. He came back with "I have no faults" I was just floored I thought he was just kidding around at first but low and behold when I turned and looked directly at him I quickly realized that no this man was serious.

Repeatedly, I asked him the same question and he did not back down. He really believed he was perfect. That man was a fanatic he was wrong, but there is and will always be someone out there that will believe in their hearts that you are beneath them. Moreover, you can be straight or gay. Remember that even when they think that they know everything ask them to answer this question. Do you know when your spirit will enter the spirit world? I think not, I have learned that we should watch and carefully think about what we are about to say because anybody can speak their own demise. Never fall prey to that type of behavior because there is nothing godly about being self-righteous. Always believing that you are right, it does not matter what kind of education or how much money you have you still cannot be right all the time. Deal wisely with believing for sure you cannot know everything. Learning to work through conflict is very important. Responding to stress in an effective way with someone that seems unbearable could be a test to those people that no matter what your approach they will not respond in a positive manner.

Years ago, I asked this young man what did it feel like to be gay? He told me that it felt like he had a female brain inside a male body. In addition, vice versa for the woman. I was amazed; I had never heard that before. African-Americans are notorious for being in denial about their son or daughter being gay. Some make excuses "His voice will change or my daughter does not dress like a boy." Well we can try to change them but sometimes we have to cut the cord. Let them run toward the wind and be themselves. The scriptures tell us that our iniquity is as filthy rags so can anyone of us point the finger of blame at Little Richard the legendary entertainer and say that he will not make it on the other side of glory! I have never met the man but I genuinely admire him because of what he had to endure. I love Little Richard honey and if I witness anyone trying to hurt him in my presence, I would surprise them by pulling a weapon out of my hair with my left hand, all the

While giving them the shock treatment with my right hand "eye for an eye". Baby a hair on his head had better not be out of place, especially if he did not do or say anything to provoke the attack. Dear beloved, I need you to conduct yourself in a professional manner, be all about business in public and play at home. When you let your guard down sometimes, that is when you become hunted prey. For example, years ago a client of mine of over two years at that time came into my place of business, she did not know it but I could feel the bad vibes from her when she walked inside. Being kind as I please, welcomed her inside then suddenly she said I am in a big hurry but I cooked a cake and I thought about you, just want to drop it off to you. Oh thank you I said, took the slice of cake tasted little piece of it being an herbalist myself. I recognized the deadly herb, when she left I took the piece of cake sliced it in little pieces sure enough that piece of cake was saturated with an herb that would have made me very sick.

Honest, a true story, I just sat there and cried because I kept asking myself "why, why, why did this person, I thought I knew so well wants to hurt me this way. Then I became very angry, I worked until closing time made sure that I found out where she lives and found her house. I waited for what seemed like hours but it was only 45 minutes. I saw her car when she drove into the driveway. I did not move a muscle, I stayed calm and cool as could be, walked up to the door rang the bell. She answered our eyes met she started shaking because I did not move, I was so upset. I do not even remember blinking I just stared at her until she started shouting I am sorry, I am sorry. I turned and left her house because I am too much of a lady to be fighting in the street, after all she knew what she had done and I never saw her again. That incident taught me a very valuable lesson people you are sometimes not aware or think will harm you in fact will hate you without a cause. Something that had never entered your mind, some will try to do to you.

America is filled with healers or haters I prefer to try to heal. Many are not happy until they see you suffering. This client attended church every Sunday, but still she was addicted to doing evil deeds. That is nothing to be proud of but when a person become bitter, I believe they will do just about anything! When I was barely twenty years old, I worked hard to fix up my apartment. Oh, I thought it was sugar sharp with my walnut furniture and this Big Giant print Bible on the coffee table, but here is the kicker when I was a child I read the bible cover to cover but I had just been just beaten over the head with the notion that I was not worthy. I actually remember feeling like what is the use I will never be good enough so each day I walked passed it tried not to notice it but it kept weighing heavily on me. My life started to change for the worst I was going through so much so one day I started back reading it and my situation did change for the best. I became aware of how many people must feel when others take it upon themselves to judge humans and yes, gay people you are good enough to read it too.

There will be some that might say who she thinks she is trying to tell us what to do. I am not trying to preach. I am trying to make a contribution to society that I feel is needed. I love big and I would like to help anyone that needs a hand. I do not like to be around stiff-necked people. In other words demented and cold-hearted people. I love to smile, motivate, encourage, anyone in any region that I live in and I have lived many places. Many church folks will continue to sit there every Sunday knowing well that they have offended someone but will never apologize. That makes me furious; I would like to shout it out! How in the hell can you even dare put your foot in the church when you cannot find it in your heart to say I am sorry. I'm woman enough to apologize to anyone and will admit when I'm wrong. America is an amazing land with many mixed up people living on it. We cannot change that but we can unlock our hearts and let the moon light in, be better human beings in the future. Parents sometimes think that their children do not know anything about life even when they are grown, but parents have

to listen also because when a Mother or Father gives respect they will get it in return or at least be willing to try to stop being so controlling. We African-Americans have a hard time and we are warriors so we like a challenge or a battle. Mother, Father, sister, or brother somebody has to show their intelligence by being the one to stop talking to keep the peace in the family. We all have to learn to let words hit us and bounce off but that takes years to develop that thick skin of tolerance. Being patient is something we must learn to practice because most Americans are just so busy running around as a chicken with the head cut off, never taking the time to meditate, watch and pray. Once a church member told me that the whole family was attending this new church because they wanted a new house and new car again that shook me up. I am thinking the Creator of the universe is not some genie out of a bottle that you can rub for and be granted wishes. Talk to the hand I said get away from me!

Since I am a serious minded person, most people misunderstand me but I am just not the one for silly foolishness. I enjoy laughter but I refuse to laugh at just anything for instance some in the entertainment business make jokes about disabled people. I will never think that is funny! Never! I remember when I was little we had a saying. I said it, I meant it, and I am here to represent it. In a way, that is what I think some gay people are trying to say they might be tired of hiding it and being so secretive. Because how can a preacher's child walk in and tell that Pastor of a huge successful church that has been preaching fire and brimstone sermons for years "Oh by the way, I'm gay." We can hide emotions but one can only pretend for so long being truthful, I think is best. Once I heard this gay church member say that their parents would have to be dead and buried before they could live free and enjoy life. I do declare that was just about the saddest thing I ever heard.

We live in times now with all this new technology that some think they have the power to do anything. I am quick to tell them "what power! What power do you have? You fish eyed fool! Only the Creator of the universe knows when the end is near or when the end will come. The scriptures Matthew chapter 24 tell us and I agree that we are living in the beginning of sorrows. Humans have been trying to predict the end since 1844 go ahead Google it.

Try not to worry about what to eat, drink or wear just be thankful for everything that you can do, like waking up each day. Walking and talking and being able to just comb your hair, since I am a caregiver and work sometimes 40 to 80 hours a week. Believe me some wish that they could do those things for themselves. Being blessed is not just about material belongings. When the power of the creator is in a person's life most often, we can clearly see it and feel it. Having love for each other in our lifetime will always be in season. If my daughter or son both were stranded on an island somewhere and the only way to reach them were to jump out of an airplane and then parachute down to earth; Honey

I am brave enough and most of all I love them both the same and unconditionally. I would gladly put my gear on, helmet, I would jump without hesitation. I would not be concerned about myself; I would be hungry for my children that I love so dear. Ask anyone that truly knows what's inside of me they will tell you. "Oh yes she will do it" if she say she's going to do it she will give it her best shot. Some people will try to abuse the love you have for them. I am here to tell you the Creator of the universe do not want you to become a Bible toting idiot/demon. Anyone that tries to use or abuse you are not to be rewarded they are to be told off, become a fighter with your wit. Show them when someone takes your kindness for weakness; show how tough you are by using your brain. Think things through before you act and believe me that takes a strong will, pray for wisdom that money cannot buy. My children are grown and doing well. I am writing with the hope that this will help another family so that they will embrace their gay son or daughter

With love and affection, because each statement of the encounters, I have written about I have experienced. I am writing and testifying about this subject from my heart to yours with tears of joy and the facts are, it can be worked out. When storms of life come and I am a living witness storms will come but even in trouble, the Creator of the universe will surround us as long as we trust and believe. Try to do our best not to forget we are all imperfect. What I believe no one else has to believe but my coping strategies did work for me. Instead of being negative about gay people, I decided to bring love to the table. When dealing with different situations in this life. The bottom line is love always finds a way. 1 Corinthians Chapter 13 Love is patient, love is kind, it does not envy, it does not boast, it is not proud, it is not rude, it is not self seeking, it is not easily angered. It keeps no record of wrongs. Love does not delight in evil but rejoices with the truth, it always protects, always trust, always hopes, always perseveres, Love never fails, and now these three remain, faith, hope and love and the greatest of these is <u>Love.</u>   The End.

www.ingramcontent.com/pod-product-compliance
Lightning Source LLC
Chambersburg PA
CBHW031335290526
45784CB00014B/2763